T0196621

FAITH BEYOND FEAR

MARLA CROOK

WESTBOW
PRESS®
A DIVISION OF THOMAS NELSON
& ZONDERVAN

WestBow Press books may be ordered through booksellers or by contacting:

WestBow Press
A Division of Thomas Nelson & Zondervan
1663 Liberty Drive
Bloomington, IN 47403
www.westbowpress.com
844-714-3454

ISBN: 978-1-6642-5094-9 (sc)
ISBN: 978-1-6642-5095-6 (e)

Library of Congress Control Number: 2021924053

Print information available on the last page.

WestBow Press rev. date: 12/23/2021

CONTENTS

DEDICATION

This book is dedicated, to my Lord and Saviour, Christ Jesus. Lord let this book be a blessing to the countless people living in fear, let it bring hope to a dying nation. Thank you for making me a light in this dark World. Thank you for leading me on this Journey to live life in the Spirit and to have daily fellowship in your presence. I would also like to thank my husband Michael, thank you for your love and the fight we have endured together. Thank you for your strength and encouragement and your continued support. To my five precious loving daughters Nicole, Alecia, Joy, Rachel, and Chareese. Thank you for your love and commitment, thank you for being the backbone of our Ministry and your continued support and dedication. I also, would like to dedicate this book to my seven grandchildren Mikayla, Madyson, Arielle, Josiah, Bella, Micah, and Chloe.

ACKNOWLEDGEMENTS

I would like to thank my church family for your prayers, support, and encouragement. Thank you for your gifts and many acts of love you have shown towards me.

FOREWORD

By Nicole Ferguson

This book will take you on a journey on how to overcome fear and live a life of absolute faith in the Almighty God, Yahweh. You are about to read an amazing book by a faithful Woman of God. Marla Crook is the most important, powerful, spiritual person in my life. She is an essence of beauty, truthfulness, boldness and kind heartedness and her love is unconditional. She has worked hard to raise five beautiful daughters and she taught us how to be strong virtuous women. Marla Crook has affected the lives of many people in so many ways. Her gratitude for God and souls has given her the power to write about her faith and her fight as a Kingdom believer. She has reached a level in life through the power of the Holy Spirit, and she can testify on how God, through her faith has allowed her to conquer many tests and trials. The challenges she has faced, has given her the victory to run this race and to keep a strong conviction of faith in the Almighty God. Thank you, Mom, for being my inspiration and the most powerful and spiritual person in my life.

INTRODUCTION

Why do we fear? Because fear is an emotion that grips our lives and causes us to wonder and become terrorized by the things we imagine. Fear is a negative impulse that causes you to look at things in your soul which is your mind. Your mind is comprised of your will, feelings, and emotions. Because we are emotional creatures, we tend to look at things in our own eyes, instead of the eyes of the Lord. Fear is a spirit, it has the power to threaten, paralyze, control; and make you doubt; it causes you to live in panic and distress. It grips your desires to look at things in the natural. It causes you to respond to thought patterns that regulate your mind to believe the worst. Fear is an unpleasant emotion caused by the belief that something is likely to cause pain or to occur. Do not allow the power of fear to destroy your life. This world has created fear in our lives. When we read the headlines in the newspaper. When we look at all the calamities and adversity and misery in life. It can cause us to react to our situations and to become complicated by the things we see and hear happening in our world. This world has caused people to panic and react to life situations through suicide and trauma attacks. The God of this world, Satan has blinded the minds of the people, through deception and frustration, which causes them to live a life of fear and uncertainty. You must rebuke the power of Satan and command fear to leave your mind do not allow the spirit of fear to keep you in bondage. You must surrender your life, to the Holy Spirit and seek the Lord through prayer and through the word of God. The Spirit of God has empowered you to live beyond the limits of fear and to live a life of victory. Fear is torment it cripples your mind and causes you to become a victim, it also causes you to live in a state of incapacitation. Do not allow the enemy through the power of darkness and demonic forces to override the power of the Holy Spirit in your life. *For God has not given us a spirit of fear, but of power and of love and of a sound mind (II Timothy 1:7 NKJV).*

CHAPTER 1
Defeat the Power of Fear in Your Mind

Fears are nothing more than a state of mind.

-Napoleon Hill

F.E.A.R. - False Evidence Appearing Real

Fear is a distressing emotion aroused by impending danger, and evil conceptions, whether the threat is real or imagined; the feeling or condition of being afraid is something that causes feelings of dread or apprehension. Fear can alarm your senses and cause you to respond on instinct. It can cause you to imagine the most dreadful thing has finally happened in your life.

Fear is a tormenting spirit that causes agony, pain, and mental suffering. It reacts to the things we encounter, things like sickness, poverty, hardship, marital problems, oppression, depression, financial problems, and fatigue.

It points out your weaknesses and causes you to lose mental strength. Fear can cause stress and anxiety. It will cause you to lose sleep, and it can affect your ability to eat and to concentrate.

Fear is a reaction that starts in the brain and spreads throughout your body. Fear can cause nervousness, panic attacks, and other illnesses in your body. Fear is capable of causing reactions in your body functions, which usually begins in your mind. Usually when you encounter a problem, the enemy will cause you to fear the outcome. Then He will cause you to become fretful and to worry because He wants to promote a sense of insecurity. Have you noticed how fear begins to set in before taking a test, going for an interview, or making a major decision? Fear can last for a brief time and pass quickly. However, anxiety and worry can last much longer and cause you to develop stress and excessive worrying until you become so irrational that you are not able to focus or think clearly.

When fear comes, you must learn how to calm your senses, relax, and refuse to panic. Because the minute that you begin to fear, it invites itself in. Once fear invades the mind, it begins to subdue you through wicked imaginations and deception.

The enemy's job is to make you believe his lies and falsehood. To cause you to live in despair, misery, and to become depressed.

There are a lot of things that can cause depression. The fear of losing a job, the fear of a losing a loved one, the fear of rejection, the fear of losing a relationship, the fear of meeting challenges in our lives, and the fear of taking on responsibilities. Sometimes people become overwhelmed by the state of fear and make their situations enormous. They may feel ashamed to discuss their problems with an outsider or family member. Whatever the circumstance may be, there is hope and a way to avoid the situation that has presented itself. Do not become anxious or frightened but stand firm and remain confident; this is just a test of your faith.

In this life, you will either live by faith or accept fear. When you live by faith, it will give you the power to believe beyond yourself and trust in a higher power. If you decide to live in fear, it will trigger excessive disturbances that could affect your physical, emotional, or psychological health.

When you live by faith and accept Christ in your life, he lives in you, and you become born again to a life of freedom and peace. As you begin this spiritual process, you start to live in a physical world and a spiritual world. Instead of living in your mind, you now begin to live in the spirit. The Holy Spirit becomes your comforter, and He starts to control you on the inside, your ability to distinguish between good and evil, light and darkness has manifested. As you maintain your authority as a Believer, you gain power to access the spiritual realms, the realms of waging war against evil forces, principalities, and powers.

Through the power of the Holy Spirit, you have power and authority to denounce every form of wickedness coming against your mind through the evil forces of darkness. You must realize that God made Satan, and he gave him authority over this Earth. God also kicked him out of heaven when he thought he could overthrow the only wise God. The Second Adam, which is Christ in you, has given you dominion to exercise all authority, through the power of prayer. You have dominion and spiritual authority to superimpose demonic forces working against your mind.

The enemy loves to attack your mind because he knows your mind is the place where your thoughts and reason comes together. You must renew your mind daily through the scriptures to develop a sound mind. Renewing your mind daily gives you power over the thoughts that bombard your mind on a constant basis. Also, you must begin to meditate on the scripture day and night. Then ask the Holy Spirit to give you the mind of Christ.

As you spend more time focusing on the power of the written Word, you will gain more power over your carnal thoughts. Your thoughts constantly love to think on things of the flesh, but the Spirit thrives on the Word of God. The enemy will continue to attack your soul, which is comprised of your feelings, your desires, and your emotions. However, with the Holy Spirit living inside you, He will give you the ability to fight your carnal thoughts.

You must train your mind to think on things that are true, pure, just, and lovely. You must constantly denounce the negative thoughts that come to your mind. This was the struggle the Apostle Paul addressed in the book of Romans. The more He wanted to follow the Spirit, *He said I see another law at work in me; waging war against the law of my mind and making me a prisoner of the law of sin at work within me (Romans 7:23 NIV).*

When God shined that bright light on Saul on the road to Damascus, he was no longer Saul; he became Paul. He said, "Who are You, Lord?" A transformation had taken place in him; he no longer was controlled by his flesh but by the Spirit. That same Spirit is leading and guiding you as you continue to follow Christ. You must stop listening to what your flesh is saying to you and speak life instead of death.

We must demolish arguments and every pretension that sets itself up against the knowledge of God and take captive every thought to make it obedient to Christ (II Corinthians 10:5 NIV). Then you will begin to develop a personal relationship with the Holy Spirit. He is the one who empowers you and gives you authority over your mind daily. The Holy Spirit is the fuel within you that enables you; it gives you the ability to fight off the power of darkness. In your prayer time, you need to ask the Holy Spirit to equip you with the seven spirits of God: the spirit of wisdom and understanding, the spirit of counsel and might, the spirit of knowledge, and the fear of the Lord. We need the Spirit of the Lord to rest on us constantly so that we can cope with the pressure and stresses of life.

The God of this world, which is Satan, wants you to rely on him instead of God. He has power and authority on this Earth to rule and reign, by Adam forfeiting His rights to Him in the garden of Eden.

Satan uses four tactics against the believer. I call it the four devices of adversity: distractions, deceptions, delays, and disappointments. He uses other people to distract and attack us. He attacks the minds of Believers by using deception to trick them into believing his lies instead of God. He tries to delay your blessings through disappointment to keep you from being committed to God. He causes havoc and complications to disappoint you and make you believe that the worst is possible.

Have you noticed the devil never gets tired of attacking Christians, but we often become weary in prayer? Satan's mission on this Earth is to corrupt and to create evil. He uses wicked forces of evil to make you doubt your Creator so that you cannot fulfill your assignment on this Earth. He wants you to believe that God is incapable of supplying your needs and desires. However, do not allow him to belittle your character and cause you to miss all God has entitled to you as a Believer. You need to take a stand and refuse Satan's deceitful tactics that attempts to deploy your mind.

You must produce a strategy to refute the opposition he will use to fight you. Please remember that Satan is a spirit, and *the weapons of our welfare are not carnal but mighty in God to pulling down strongholds (II Corinthians 10:5 KJV)*. Your mind is a stronghold that the enemy fights continually. You must depend on the Word of God. Tell the enemy to take his hands off your mind. The Word is your defense; trust it, pray it, and speak it daily. The power of the written Word has given you power and authority to speak life to every dead situation. You have power in your mouth to command fear and panic to leave your spiritual house. Your battle is in your mind; resist the spirits that are talking to your mind.

CHAPTER 2
Fight the Enemy Who Is Attacking You

He who is not every day, conquering fear
has not learned the secret of life.

—*Ralph Waldo Emerson*

In the midst, of every battle, you must learn how to fight back. Have you ever wondered why David did not lose many battles? It is because David chose to focus on how big God was. He did not depend on his strength, but he relied on the strength of God. The Word says it is *God who arms me with strength and makes my way perfect (Psalm 18:32 NKJV).*

David knew that God was able to deliver him, because he had remembered every victory, and how God had fought for him. Your previous victories should make you depend on God even more. When you realize that the battle is not yours, it belongs to God.

David was fighting what was coming against him. He could see what he was fighting. The bible says we are fighting against spiritual wickedness against principalities, against powers, against darkness, spirits without bodies assigned to frustrate your spirit. You are fighting demonic forces of evil such as witches, warlocks, Satanists, familiar spirits, witchcraft, wizards, generational curses, leviathan spirits, jezebel spirits, and occult spirits, and the lists goes on.

In this world of visible and invisible forces you must learn how to war in the spiritual realm against these unseen spirits, which are warring against your soulish man. You must come to grips with yourself that this is a spiritual battle with unknown foes waging war against you.

The question is what are using to fight with? Every challenge is a fight, David knew God would rescue him because he had rescued him before. He trusted in the faith of God. He trusted that he already had the victory, he strengthened himself. David said, "I defeated a lion and a bear, so who are you, to cause me to fear you uncircumcised giant." David had faced opposition, but he realized that God was within me. Every opposition is preparation for a greater battle.

Realize that the same God that brought David through is still fighting with you. Every battle you must face is a battle of complete victory. Victory only comes to those who refuse to lose. An attack is a spiritual warfare and the only way you win is by fighting back. David used a sling shot, but you must use your mouth.

The Word of God says life and death are in the power of the tongue. You have been empowered to speak life and pronounce doom on your enemy. You must become a Warrior if you plan on winning.

It is time for you to mount up in the Spirit and realize that no weapon formed against you shall prosper, stand firm on the promises of God. Begin to use your mouth and speak the Word of God with power and authority, bind up the spirits and loose every demonic force against your mind.

Let the enemy know that is enough, let him know that you refuse to settle for less. You must pray against the strongman and pull down every stronghold. You say what is a stronghold?

It is an area of darkness within your mind that causes you to struggle with thoughts, emotions, and habits that wage war against your relationship with Christ. This battle within your mind tries to distort the truth to confuse your way of thinking. Satan is the father of lies so you know that every form of evil is rooted from darkness.

You must walk in the fullness of the word of truth to guard your heart and mind from His attacks. Every spiritual attack comes in various forms through people, circumstances, situations, and opinions.

You must engage your mind, through the Holy Spirit and invoke the presence of God to invade the territory of the enemy that is working behind the scenes to hinder your progress. Stand firm on the promises of God and cancel every arrow of interference that the enemy will try to use against your mind. release the Angels of God to fight on your behalf and maintain your joy, *Do not sorrow,* for *the joy of the Lord is your strength. (Nehemiah 8:10 NKJV)*

CHAPTER 3
The Test of Fear

Without fear there cannot be courage.

-Christopher Paolini

Fear is a spirit that looks to torment and traumatize a victim. When fear sets in it begins to confuse and frustrate your mind to think the worst. It causes you to believe that there is no way out of the situation. It captures your feelings and your human emotions. When Adam and Eve ate the fruit in the Garden of Eden. They faced fear, because they knew that they had disobeyed God, so they hid themselves from God. When Cain killed Abel, he was afraid because he allowed angry to override his fear. So, instead of pleading with God he decided to kill his brother. We are all equipped with the survival instincts necessary to respond with fear when we sense danger or feel unsafe.

It is the adamic nature that causes us to fear. When God created man in his image, man did not fear because he was formed in his likeness, but after he sinned, he became just like you and me. He was able to recognize good from evil.

Fear is a learned behavior that we respond to as infants. The fear of your mother leaving you at daycare. The fear of sleeping in a dark room or trusting someone.

As growing up as a child the fear of insects. Fear has been here since the beginning of time. However, the bible says *"Fear not, for I am with you be not dismayed for I am your God (Isaiah 41:10 NKJV).*

Throughout the bible we see people who endured difficult battles of fear. Moses had to face Pharaoh. Esther had to face the king. She put all her maidens on fast and she was determined to go to the King, she said if I perish, I perish. Joseph had to face his brothers and uncertain circumstances wondering if they would recognize his face. And Joseph said to his brothers, please come near to me so they came near to him then he said, "I am Joseph your brother, who you sold into Egypt". *But now, do not therefore be grieved or angry with yourselves because you sold me here; for God sent me before you to preserve life (Genesis 45:4-5 NKJV).* Joseph's test was a test of courage and fear, but he overcame.

You may feel like Gideon in the bible, the least in your household. When the Angel of the Lord appeared to him, he said Mighty man of Valor. You shall save Israel from the Midianites, and you shall defeat them unanimously. In Gideon's mind this would be a challenging task to carry out.

How could he defeat his enemies as one man? The Lord said to him go in my might and you will save Israel from the Midianites, for I am sending you.

When the Angel appeared to him to his surprise, he was amazed to hear the Angel call him a Man of Mighty Valor. His first response was how can I deliver my people, because within his mind he was looking at his background. Sometimes the failures we have seen within our families can cause us to believe that we are incapable of becoming a success. The fear of becoming successful can overwhelm our mind and cause us not to believe in ourselves.

However, he obeyed the Angel and although fear overwhelmed him, he took men with him by night and torn down the altar of Baal.

The next morning, they inquired and asked who has done this thing. They replied that the son of Gideon has done this thing. Then the men of the city called for his father, Josiah and said bring your son out he must die. Can you imagine how Gideon felted to know the thing he feared was about to take place simply because he obeyed. His father said all who stand against Gideon will plead for Baal. If you plead for Baal, you will die by morning. He said if Baal is God let him plead for himself. When Gideon responded they called him Jerubbaal.

He sounded the trumpet of alarm and had twenty thousand men to join him in battle. However, He ended up with only three hundred men. Gideon won the battle with torches, pitchers, and trumpets. The memory of this great deliverance impressed itself on the mind of nations.

It proves to show no matter how hard it may seem to you. When you overcome the spirit of fear you can win any battle.

Do not allow the enemy of your mind to cause you back down, on your belief.

Take a stand and fight against whatever is fighting against you. The word says you are more than a conqueror, put on your armor and fight the good fight of faith.

Do not continue to allow the spirit of fear to keep your mind in bondage. Learn to pray against the prince of the power of the air. Fear should never cause you take down, when you need to take a stand. When you change your mindset and depend on the Holy Spirit. He will give you power to destroy these spirits coming against your mind.

The Holy Spirit will give you power and authority over any spirit. He wants to work on your behalf, invite him into your heart right now. When you pray the Holy Spirit is present to take your request to your Heavenly Father.

People are afraid to face tomorrow because they fear the uncertainty of life. Countless marriages are destroyed because of fear. Youths are running away from home because of fear. Families are being destroyed because of fear.

We constantly live in a society where fear is the norm. Bosses exercising their authority and making threats, causing people to lose their jobs because of fear.

So how do you escape their power of fear? You must refuse to be a Victim and become a Victor!!!!

I have seen so many people crippled by this spirit, helpless, confused, and troubled. They do not know whether to fight or just give in to it.

In the bible we see many accounts of people just like ourselves afraid of the enemy.

After Jacob had worked for twenty-one years for his uncle. He had to return home to meet his brother.

In his mind, he was saying how can I face my past because he had stolen his brother's birthright. The night after he had prayed, he had fought with an Angel. The Angel wrestled with him all night. By the break of dawn, he realized he was fighting a losing battle. However, Jacob was determined to defeat the fear within his mind. When he finally met his brother, his brother blessed him and told him he had forgiven him.

Sometimes you must endure tremendous pressure, but do not allow your mind to reason with your flesh. The God of his world has blinded the minds of people. He is causing people to commit suicide, to die prematurely. The enemy is testing your character, he wants you to give in to him. However, you must refuse to remain a prey to the spirit of fear, do not allow Satan to overthrow your mind with his wicked devices.

Become aware and plan a strategy against the perils of the enemy and demolish his tactics against your mind. You must guard your heart and mind and set up barriers to confine the spirits working against your mindset. The power you possess as a believer as sustained you to keep a positive mind. Be strong and courageous and hope to the end.

CHAPTER 4
Fear I Command You to Go

Find Peace in where and what you are.

-Christopher Paolini

When you make a command, you must stand your ground and mean what you say. You must release the power of your words into the atmosphere and invoke the presence of God. Fear only poses a threat to those who are compelled by the sudden disturbances of the advances against your mind. Fear is also a tormenting and holding spirit caused by the evil one. That causes you to become afraid of impending circumstances or situations enforced through the enemy. It attacks your feelings, your emotions, and your state of being, forcing your mind to panic and become overwhelmed.

Your mind then begins to race and your pulse elevates to a level as if you are having an anxiety attack. Fear will cause you to response in a way you never thought you would. You must be willing to face your fears and ask the Holy Spirit to give you power to resist every demonic grip of the enemy.

I can remember having to face demanding situations not knowing the outcome. Yet trying to remain calm, in the face of adversity. If I only had relied on God instead of my human mind, the problem could have been avoided. However, looking at the situation in my own eyes it caused me to rely on my human instinct. Sometimes your instincts can produce negative impulses and cause you more hardship than what you anticipated. You must maintain a good attitude. Anytime a problem arises you should use Godly wisdom and a sound mind and begin to exercise your faith. The minute fear manifest, it arouses all your senses and causes you to panic.

Once you panic and the enemy detects it, then he will begin to try to manipulate your mind. You must strategize, look at the circumstances, and begin to pray and ask the Lord what you need to do.

Sometimes in your tests or trials the Lord is trying to develop his character within you. The test is to see just how far you are willing to go. When you keep a cheerful outlook and persevere in the Spirit you will navigate through every obstacle. Because we live in a world full of darkness and wickedness, and you have many adversaries working behind the scenes to try to hinder your progress. The Word says that *the weapons of our warfare are not carnal, but mighty in God for the pulling down strongholds, casting down arguments and every high thing that exalts itself against the knowledge of God, bringing every thought into captivity to the obedience of Christ (II Corinthians 10:4-5NKJV)*. Your adversity the devil walks about like a roaring Lion. The Word did not say he was a Lion, he said he walks like he is a Lion. He wants you to believe he is a Lion so he can intimidate you. He wants you to denounce the faith, so you can live a life of defeat.

The Apostle Paul had many battles to conquer, they hid him in a basket. He was threatened, he was shipwrecked, even a snake tried to bite him; but he shook it off.

When you have the faith in the Almighty God, his faith succeeds the fear of this World. Every challenge you may be facing now is greater than your situation. The Word of God says greater is He that is in you than he that is in the world. The problems and obstacles you are facing is just a detour to stop you from fulfilling your destiny on this Earth. The power He has invested within your spirit is far beyond the fear that grips and snares your soul. You are a vessel for the Holy Spirit, and no weapon formed against you shall prosper. So, continue to command the enemy to take his hands off your mind, and remember to stand firm on the solid rock which is Christ. The Word of God, is your defense rely on it, pray it, and speak it daily. The power of the written word has granted you power and authority to speak life to every dead situation.

You have all authority and dominion, so use your mouth and command fear to leave your house. Do not allow the enemy to helm you up in a corner. The battle is in your mind, resist the spirit of fear and it will flee.

CHAPTER 5
Speak to the Fear

Fear defeats more people than any other thing in the world.

-Ralph Waldo Emerson

Fear is a tool that Satan uses against a believer you must choose to live without fear. You must tell fear to leave your mind. Speak to the fear, name the fear, and resist the enemy causing you to fear. The bible says *There is no fear in love; but perfect love casts out fear (I John 4:18 NKJV)* remember that fear is torment. Anytime you distressed by fear you must face it head-on. The enemy loves to intimidate your mind and cause you to accept the fear. You must continually denounce it and cancel every attack the adversary presents.

Then Jesus was led up by the Spirit in the wilderness the devil used many attempts against him, he said if you be the Son of God command this stone to be bread, but He answered and said, man should not live by bread alone, but by every word of God (Matthew 4:4 NKJV).

Then he took him to a high mountain and showed him all the kingdoms of the world. And the devil said to him all this authority will I give to you. If you would bow down and worship before me. But he did not realize that Jesus had a kingdom of his own. He continued to attack him, to try to discredit him, but with every test he failed.

Each time he told Jesus if you be the Son of God, he was trying to make Jesus deny his lordship. He tried to dematerialize his senses to make him doubt that he was truly the Son of God. Finally, Jesus told him you shall not tempt the Lord your God. Satan thought he was dealing with an amateur, however he found out that he was dealing with God. So, beware of your adversity Satan, because he is sitting back studying your speech. He is watching your behavior and your motives waiting on the right opportunity to attack you, your children, and your spouse.

When you learn how to resist him, he will flee, Satan is a coward and most times he will back down, most of the time he is just trying to see if you are going to fight back. However, in any battle you must draw the line and use your weapon. Do you know? your weapon is your mouth, and the Word of God is your defense.

The bible says the Word of God is powerful and sharper than a two- edged sword. It has the ability, to destroy yokes and break chains of bondage,

The enemy that is attacking you may be a physical creature, or it may be spiritual, but the power of the Word of God will always prevail. *You are not fighting against flesh and blood, but against principalities, against powers; against the rulers of darkness of this age; against spiritual host of wickedness in the heavenly places. (Ephesians 6:12 KJV).*

When Jacob wrestled with an invisible spirit, he never knew it was an Angel he thought he was wrestling against God. However, he was determined not to give up, he said I am not going to let you go until you bless me. Sometimes the thing you are fighting is yourself.

The enemy knows your destiny and he is trying to deny you access to the promise of your inheritance. He will use everything in his power to make you give up and give into the schemes of Satan. As a soldier equipped for battle you must remain committed, persistent, consistent, and dedicated to the call.

You must hold fast to your belief and do not waver. You must shame the enemy and deny him his rights. Do not allow fear to rob you of your joy, because fear is self-rooted it can only grip you if you let it.

You must girt up the lions of your mind and hope until the end. Tell the enemy I denounce every tactic you are using, and continually refuse the voices that are talking to your mind. The voices you hear want to intimidate you so you will give in and get weary. The voices you hear are like a bully that continues to make threats until you stand up to him.

In any battle you must counteract the forces of evil that are constantly coming against your mind. The bible *says the Kingdom of God suffers violent, but the violent are taking it by force (Matthew 11:12 NKJV).* Every blunt trauma the enemy is using, you must resist the blows and stand strong. The battle is not yours it is the Lord's.

Your War Angels are fighting for you, they are waging war in the Spirit against these principalities and powers. Whenever you are in heated battle you must press against the forces that are pressing against you. Do not settle for defeat but fight until the end. Prayer is your weapon so continue to pray until you get a breakthrough.

CHAPTER 6
Developing a Sound Mind

A positive mindset can overcome any obstacle

-Roger Lee

In the midst, of all that is taking place you can keep an inner peace and joyful state of mind. The word says let not your heart be troubled, neither let it be afraid. When you are afraid you are not trusting God. The world is full of confusion, but you can still have the peace of knowing that whatever takes place I know God is abiding within me. Peace is like a stream that continues to flow. The Holy Spirit is your peace, He is your comforter and no matter what is troubling your spirit. He will always be there to help you to keep a sound mind. Having a sound mind requires diligence, it will constrain you to be careful and mindful of the Word of God. It begins to direct your emotions and senses to line up with the power of the written word. The word gives you the ability to speak life and not death.

When you speak death, the enemy uses your own words to curse you, but when you speak life, your words create power.

The bible says *a wholesome tongue is a tree of life, but perverseness in it breaks the spirit (Proverbs 15:4 NKJV)*

The more you speak power words into the atmosphere is the greater success you will have. You have power and authority to walk in dominion.

Cultivating a sound mind begins with using your wisdom. When you walk and live in the wisdom of God. You feel his presence surrounding your mind. Your mind must become programmed to think different. Your soulish man loves to think on things of the world. However, your spiritual man thinks on how you can live a holy and separated life for Christ. Living for Christ requires faithfulness and obedience. Obedience will cause you to hunger for the essence of his word and faithfulness rewards your obedience. Sometimes you can be willing but not obedient. Being willing affords you the ability to hear and listen to the Holy Spirit. Throughout the bible you hear of many people failing because they simply did not listen and take heed to the voice of God.

When God told the Prophet Jonah to go to Nineveh and cry out against the wickedness in that city he refused and got on a ship going in the opposite direction. He turned down the assignment and became rebellious because he did not want to go and preach repentance to stubborn and stout-hearted people.

Instead, he got on a boat to Tarshish, angry and discouraged. However, God caused the boat and the wind on the sea to become tempest. When the crew searched for Jonah, they found him sleep. They decided to cast lots to see who was causing the disturbance. The lot fell on Jonah, so they cast him overboard. Jonah did not realize that his disobedience had caused him great hardship. He found himself in the belly of the fish. He cried out to God because he realized then that God was serious about his instruction.

Do not allow the enemy to cause you to miss the mark because of your disobedience. Obedience is always better than a sacrifice. Living a separated life for the Lord requires discipline, and discipline requires dedication and dedication will cause you to become elevated to a place of promotion. However, keeping a sound mind will cause you to soar in the Spirit, through daily meditation of the word.

The more power you give your mind to think on negative thoughts is the longer it will take for you to develop a sound mind. Your mind can go all the way back to your childhood. It can remember the past, and the present, but your mind never seems to reflect on the future.

Your mind can remember all the hurtful things, but it never seems to look at the positive things which you have achieved. To become successful, you must give your mind constantly to the word of God.

The word gives insight into the future, it motivates your efforts, it promotes your thought life and develops your character. Living in character will help you to reflect your identity and your purpose. It is often easy to find a person who lives on purpose, because they will always keep a strong mindset. This type of person constantly lives by faith and not by fear. If you are the type of person who always finds excuses and never solutions, it means you are living in fear. On the other hand, if you are the type of person who produces innovative ideas, and promotes others and has a hopeful attitude, then you are a person who lives by faith.

When you walk in faith you know that all things work together for those who love the Lord.

When you constantly depend on living a righteous life. You begin to practice your faith by your actions.

You start to develop a steadfast hope and a sound mind. You also begin to offset the enemy that is coming against your mind, remember a carnal mind is the devil's workshop. As a Christian you must deprogram your mind and pull down the carnal thoughts that cloud your mind. Because every thought that comes to your mind gives you a choice to decide.

The decisions you make can cause you to live in doubt or failure. But if you live and strive for purpose you will succeed. Many people fail in life because they are convinced in their own mind through the schemes of Satan, instead of depending on the Holy Spirit.

Some decisions you have made has wrecked your life, because you went on your feelings and your emotions. When you are led by the Holy Spirit, he will lead and guide your thoughts. The Spirit of God will give you the ability to discern what is best for your situation.

So, stay focused and stay on track and always seek the Lord on any major decision you must make. Do not be tossed and driven by the cares of this world. Choose to be positive and strive for perfection. The world is full of empty minded people because the God of this world has blinded the minds of the people.

The bible says you must guard your heart and mind and beware of evil doers. Continue to stand on the promises of God and remain confident. Be alert and vigilant, resist the devil and he will flee.

CHAPTER 7
Faith over Fear

He who is not every day conquering some fear
has not learned the secret of Life

-Ralph Waldo Emerson

D o you have a steadfast faith? or have you allowed fear to overpower your state of being. *Faith is the substance of things hope for, the evidence of things not seen (Hebrews 12:1 KJV).* Your faith will give you the power to believe for the unseen and to live in the supernatural. However, fear will cause unbelief and doubt. You must realize no matter what has happened to you in the past. Your faith in the almighty God is your highest reward. Faith is not knowing the outcome, but faith is believing it is already done. Fear is looking at the circumstance and yet doubting whether it is possible. The Apostle Paul said, *I have fought a good fight, I have finished my course, and I have kept the faith (ll Timothy 4:7 NKJV).* Paul's faith in God won him the victory. Whenever your faith is tested, do not waver but hope to the end.

Always remember the battle is not yours but the Lord's. I have never read in the bible where God lost a battle. So, every victory is yours if you can only believe it. Victory means triumph, it means the power that the enemy possessed has been destroyed. The victory you manifest depends on the faith that you own. Your faith is a test of your belief.

The bible says the just shall live by faith, when you are living by faith it is no longer you, it is a higher power. When the woman who had been sick for twelve years came and she touched the hem of Jesus garment. She was set free, because she believed. Her faith made her whole because she trusted in the healer and not the doctor. Instantly, she became healed from her blood disease. Another man came unto Jesus lying on a bed he was a paralytic he had a rare disease he could not walk. When he saw his faith, He said *Son be of a good cheer your sins are forgiven you (Matthew 9:2 NKJV).*

When you have the faith to step out on nothing, God is a big enough God to back you up. I have seen countless people healed of diverse types of sicknesses and diseases.

In the book of Hebrews, you can read about all the Heroes of faith, the bible says These all died in faith, not having received the promises but seen them afar off were assured of them and confessed that they were strangers and pilgrims on the earth (Hebrews 11:13 NKJV). These Heroes only believed even though their faith was tested they Had a testimony that was pleasing unto God.

Your trust is your belief ... *Now to him who is able to do exceedingly abundantly above all we can ask or think, according to the power that works in us (Ephesians 3:20 NKJV).* The power you own is working in you to manifest the miracle you are looking for. The only thing you need to do is stand on the promises of God.

The word of God is his promise, and he cannot deny himself. If He spoke it, His word shall come to pass. Faith is action, the word you speak is voice activated, when you speak words into the atmosphere it creates power, and they create change. When God commanded the light to appear out of darkness, immediately the darkness disappeared. He spoke and the energy of the power of his voice caused a shift in the atmosphere. Because light is energy, light has frequency that moves by sound and light travels faster than sound. So, when God spoke the waves of sound created a friction to carry his words and cause movement in the air. Because you are a believer, making you an heir and a joint heir with Christ. You also possess the power to speak the word into the atmosphere and to create a change in your environment. You have power and authority to execute and legislate your jurisdictional power on Earth through signs, wonders, and miracles through the supernatural realm of the spirit of God.

In the bible, I remember when the king of Israel sent his army against the Prophet Elisha and the army surrounded his house with horses and chariots. His servant came running to him afraid, but Elisha began to pray and commanded his servant's eyes to come open. The he spoke, those with us are more than whose who are with them.

Elisha had faith in his God through the mighty works he saw through his master Elijah. He had received the mantle of his master and he had also received a double portion of his spirit. He only needed to rely on the faith of God to see the manifestation of the glory of God.

The power you own as a king and a priest on this Earth has given you the ability to reign and rule your domain and to decree and declare what you want to see.

When you exercise your faith, it is complete. The only thing you have do, is take him at his word. Do not allow your mind to hold you back, launch out in the deep and trust God.

Many people are in despair because they do not realize what a mighty God we serve. They have let the god of this world paralyze their mind, and they have given up theirs rights as a believer through their unbelief. When you accept Jesus Christ in your life you give him the authority to lead and guide your life. Your faith in him will subdue all the powers of this world. It will give you the power and strength to fight and keep a position as a champion.

Every champion has to fight, and every fight is a fight of faith. So, it is time for you to mount up with wings like eagles to run and not be weary and to walk and not faint. Your opponent is no longer fear, but absolute faith in the Almighty God.

Your faith in God will bring you through any storm, your faith in God will take you on a journey far beyond your own imagination. It will cause you to trust in what you cannot fathom. It will lead you to a place of conviction to go beyond your mere senses. It will cause you to see the supernatural power of God through countless miracles and signs and wonders. The bible says *for we walk by faith and not by sight (ll Corinthians 5:7 NKJV)*. Faith is the surmountable assurance of God.

CHAPTER 8
Victory through the Cross

Faith is the strength by which a shattered world
shall emerge into the light.

-Helen Keller

The power of fear is aborted, and the enemy has is destroyed. The test of your fear has finally ended. Your faith has succeeded, and you have overcome, now you have the power to stand strong in faith. You are victorious, you have waged war against the enemy who was waging war against your mind.

The Holy Spirit within you has given you the victory and you now can believe that all things are possible to him who only believes. You have endured the battle, the war the enemy waged against you is over you are an overcomer you are more than a conqueror. The victory that Jesus won for us on the cross has granted you power to live a victorious life.

When Jesus was on the cross, he already had won the battle because he had faith in his Father. He told one of the thieves on the cross, this day you shall be with me in Paradise. His faith in his Father gave him the victory to defeat his enemies and to endure every affliction,

When they placed him in the tomb, God sent his Angels to roll the stone away. When he appeared to Mary, He told her not to touch him because he had to make his blood report to the father. Then he told her to go tell his disciples to meet him in Jerusalem. They were in fear, but he had already assured them that he would return. He told them to go to the upper room and stay there and wait on the Spirit that he had promised them. When the Spirit came in the form of a rushing mighty wind it filled everyone in the room. They had already received a touch of Holy Spirit when he had breathed on them.

Then they all begin to speak in new tongues as the Spirit descended on them. When people on the outside noticed them, they thought they were drunk.

The authority they received gave them power, and they no longer had to trust in fear. Their faith had won them the victory.

Christ Jesus fought the ultimate battle, and he won the victory for all humanity. He defeated the cross, death, and hell. He enabled you and me to live in a world, where fear was the norm. But now you have permission and immunity to live in a world free from sin and free from the demonic plights of fear.

You can now decree and declare that fear has no place in your mind. Where fear was ruling your mind, you can now denounce every thought and let Satan know you have conquered his evil plot. Your life is now a testimony for someone else. You are a shining light that can never be hid, a candle put on a candlestick that gives light to the hearts of others.

Your trust in the Almighty God has given you the faith to stand on the promises of God.

Fear no longer has dominion over you. The victory of the cross has given you the power to raise your voice against all fear. The enemy is destroyed, and God is exalted. Lift your hands now … and tell fear you are a defeated foe. Tell fear you can no longer paralyze my thoughts. Let fear know that you are no longer a victim of despair and anxiety. Let fear know you are more than a conqueror and that no weapon formed against you shall ever prosper.

The Word of God is your defense against the spiritual attacks and the unseen forces of darkness that was waging war against you. The Faith you now own can subdue any evil force. You live in Kingdom that cannot be shaken. His Kingdom is an everlasting Kingdom that shall reign forever on this Earth.

The battle in hell was conquered, Christ became the victor to give us victory over death, hell, and the grave. You must refuse to allow the enemy to advance on your territory. You have all power and spiritual authority to strategize and head off every plan and plot.

You can now, denounce that fear and command the enemy to get out of your house. Put on the whole armor of God because you are now able to stand against all the wiles of the devil, stand therefore, having your loins girt about with truth, and having on the breastplate of righteousness, and your feet shod with the preparation of the gospel of peace, above all taking the shield of faith, wherewith you shall be able to quench all the fiery darts of the wicked. (*Ephesians 6:11-16 paraphased*) Nothing can defeat you NOW!!!! the potential you own has power to overcome any battle or obstacle.

The Victory is Won!!!! the battle has been fought, now declare, and take back what belongs to you.

DELIVERANCE PRAYER
TO OVERCOME FEAR

Heavenly Father, In the name of Jesus, your Word says that you did not give me the spirit of fear, but of power, and of love and of a sound mind. Lord, through the power of your Word you said you have given me all authority to denounce all fear. I bind the spirit of fear that has held my mind in bondage, and I command it out, by the power of the blood of Christ. I release the power of the Holy Spirit to take authority over every fear that has tormented my mind since childhood.

I curse every generational curse brought upon my life through my lineage. Satan the Lord rebuke you, I refuse to be a victim to you. I command every fear of intimidation to lose my mind right now.

Father, I assign your Angelic hosts to cancel and demolish every stronghold of fear that has held me in bondage. I refuse to be a victim of fear, for Lord, you have granted me immunity through your Son Christ Jesus. I command every demonic and satanic attack of the enemy to release my mind. I now accept my new life in Christ Jesus. Thank you Lord, for total freedom.

Printed in the United States
by Baker & Taylor Publisher Services